Great Works

Instructional Guides for Literature

If You Give...
Series Guide

A guide for the books by Laura Numeroff
Great Works Author: Tracy Pearce

SHELL EDUCATION

Publishing Credits

Corinne Burton, M.A.Ed., *President*; Owen Pearce, *Contributing Author*; Emily R. Smith, M.A.Ed., *Editorial Director*; Lee Aucoin, *Multimedia Designer*; Stephanie Bernard, *Assistant Editor*; Don Tran, *Production Artist*; Amber Goff, *Editorial Assistant*

Image Credits

Shutterstock (cover)

Standards

© 2007 Teachers of English to Speakers of Other Languages, Inc. (TESOL)
© 2007 Board of Regents of the University of Wisconsin System. World-Class Instructional Design and Assessment (WIDA)
© Copyright 2010. National Governors Association Center for Best Practices and Council of Chief State School Officers. All rights reserved.

Shell Education
5301 Oceanus Drive
Huntington Beach, CA 92649-1030
http://www.shelleducation.com
ISBN 978-1-4807-6991-5
© 2015 Shell Educational Publishing, Inc.

Table of contents

How to Use This Literature Guide

Today's standards demand rigor and relevance in the reading of complex texts. The units in this series guide teachers in a rich and deep exploration of worthwhile works of literature for classroom study. The most rigorous instruction can also be interesting and engaging!

Many current strategies for effective literacy instruction have been incorporated into these instructional guides for literature. Throughout the units, text-dependent questions are used to determine comprehension of the book as well as student interpretation of the vocabulary words. The books chosen for the series are complex and are exemplars of carefully crafted works of literature. Close reading is used throughout the units to guide students toward revisiting the text and using textual evidence to respond to prompts orally and in writing. Students must analyze the story elements in multiple assignments for each section of the book. All of these strategies work together to rigorously guide students through their study of literature.

The next few pages describe how to use this guide for a purposeful and meaningful literature study. Each section of this guide is set up in the same way to make it easier for you to implement the instruction in your classroom.

Theme Thoughts

The great works of literature used throughout this series have important themes that have been relevant to people for many years. Many of the themes will be discussed during the various sections of this instructional guide. However, it would also benefit students to have independent time to think about the key themes of the book.

Before students begin reading, have them complete the *Pre-Reading Theme Thoughts* (page 13). This graphic organizer will allow students to think about the themes outside the context of the story. They'll have the opportunity to evaluate statements based on important themes and defend their opinions. Be sure to keep students' papers for comparison to the *Post-Reading Theme Thoughts* (page 60). This graphic organizer is similar to the pre-reading activity. However, this time, students will be answering the questions from the point of view of one of the characters in the book. They have to think about how the character would feel about each statement and defend their thoughts. To conclude the activity, have students compare what they thought about the themes before they read the book to what the characters discovered during the story.

How to Use This Literature Guide (cont.)

Vocabulary

Each teacher reference vocabulary overview page has definitions and sentences about how key vocabulary words are used in the section. These words should be introduced and discussed with students. Students will use these words in different activities throughout the book.

On some of the vocabulary student pages, students are asked to answer text-related questions about vocabulary words from the sections. The following question stems will help you create your own vocabulary questions if you'd like to extend the discussion.

- How does this word describe _____'s character?
- How does this word connect to the problem in this story?
- How does this word help you understand the setting?
- Tell me how this word connects to the main idea of this story.
- What visual pictures does this word bring to your mind?
- Why do you think the author used this word?

At times, you may find that more work with the words will help students understand their meanings and importance. These quick vocabulary activities are a good way to further study the words.

- Students can play vocabulary concentration. Make one set of cards that has the words on them and another set with the definitions. Then, have students lay them out on the table and play concentration. The goal of the game is to match vocabulary words with their definitions. For early readers or English language learners, the two sets of cards could be the words and pictures of the words.

- Students can create word journal entries about the words. Students choose words they think are important and then describe why they think each word is important within the book. Early readers or English language learners could instead draw pictures about the words in a journal.

- Students can create puppets and use them to act out the vocabulary words from the stories. Students may also enjoy telling their own character-driven stories using vocabulary words from the original stories.

How to Use This Literature Guide (cont.)

Analyzing the Literature

After you have read each section with students, hold a small-group or whole-class discussion. Provided on the teacher reference page for each section are leveled questions. The questions are written at two levels of complexity to allow you to decide which questions best meet the needs of your students. The Level 1 questions are typically less abstract than the Level 2 questions. These questions are focused on the various story elements, such as character, setting, and plot. Be sure to add further questions as your students discuss what they've read. For each question, a few key points are provided for your reference as you discuss the book with students.

Reader Response

In today's classrooms, there are often great readers who are below average writers. So much time and energy is spent in classrooms getting students to read on grade level that little time is left to focus on writing skills. To help teachers include more writing in their daily literacy instruction, each section of this guide has a literature-based reader response prompt. Each of the three genres of writing is used in the reader responses within this guide: narrative, informative/explanatory, and opinion. Before students write, you may want to allow them time to draw pictures related to the topic. Book-themed writing paper is provided on page 70 if your students need more space to write.

Guided Close Reading

Within the each section of this guide, it is suggested that you closely reread a portion of the text with your students. The sections to be reread are described by location within the story since there are no page numbers in these books. After rereading the section, there are a few text-dependent questions to be answered by students.

Working space has been provided to help students prepare for the group discussion. They should record their thoughts and ideas on the activity page and refer to it during your discussion. Rather than just taking notes, you may want to require students to write complete responses to the questions before discussing them with you.

Encourage students to read one question at a time and then go back to the text and discover the answer. Work with students to ensure that they use the text to determine their answers rather than making unsupported inferences. Suggested answers are provided in the answer key.

How to Use This Literature Guide (cont.)

Guided close Reading (cont.)

The generic open-ended stems below can be used to write your own text-dependent questions if you would like to give students more practice.

- What words in the story support . . . ?
- What text helps you understand . . . ?
- Use the book to tell why _____ happens.
- Based on the events in the story, . . . ?
- Show me the part in the text that supports . . . .
- Use the text to tell why . . . .

Making connections

The activities in this section help students make cross-curricular connections to mathematics, science, social studies, fine arts, or other curricular areas. These activities require higher-order thinking skills from students but also allow for creative thinking.

Language Learning

A special section has been set aside to connect the literature to language conventions. Through these activities, students will have opportunities to practice the conventions of standard English grammar, usage, capitalization, and punctuation.

story Elements

It is important to spend time discussing what the common story elements are in literature. Understanding the characters, setting, plot, and theme can increase students' comprehension and appreciation of the story. If teachers begin discussing these elements in early childhood, students will more likely internalize the concepts and look for the elements in their independent reading. Another very important reason for focusing on the story elements is that students will be better writers if they think about how the stories they read are constructed.

In the story elements activities, students are asked to create work related to the characters, setting, or plot. Consider having students complete only one of these activities. If you give students a choice on this assignment, each student can decide to complete the activity that most appeals to him or her. Different intelligences are used so that the activities are diverse and interesting to all students.

How to Use This Literature Guide (cont.)

Culminating Activity

At the end of this instructional guide is a creative culminating activity that allows students the opportunity to share what they've learned from reading the book. This activity is open ended so that students can push themselves to create their own great works within your language arts classroom.

Comprehension Assessment

The questions in this section require students to think about the book they've read as well as the words that were used in the book. Some questions are tied to quotations from the book to engage students and require them to think about the text as they answer the questions.

Response to Literature

Finally, students are asked to respond to the literature by drawing pictures and writing about the characters and stories. A suggested rubric is provided for teacher reference.

Correlation to the Standards

Shell Education is committed to producing educational materials that are research and standards based. As part of this effort, we have correlated all of our products to the academic standards of all 50 states, the District of Columbia, the Department of Defense Dependents Schools, and all Canadian provinces.

Purpose and Intent of Standards

Standards are designed to focus instruction and guide adoption of curricula. Standards are statements that describe the criteria necessary for students to meet specific academic goals. They define the knowledge, skills, and content students should acquire at each level. Standards are also used to develop standardized tests to evaluate students' academic progress. Teachers are required to demonstrate how their lessons meet standards. Standards are used in the development of all of our products, so educators can be assured they meet high academic standards.

How to Find Standards Correlations

To print a customized correlation report of this product for your state, visit our website at http://www.shelleducation.com and follow the online directions. If you require assistance in printing correlation reports, please contact our Customer Service Department at 1-877-777-3450.

correlation to the standards (cont.)

standards correlation chart

The lessons in this book were written to support today's college and career readiness standards. The following chart indicates which lessons address each standard.

College and Career Readiness Standard	Section
Read closely to determine what the text says explicitly and to make logical inferences from it; cite specific textual evidence when writing or speaking to support conclusions drawn from the text. (R.1)	Analyzing the Literature Sections 1–5; Guided Close Reading Sections 1–5; Making Connections Sections 3, 5; Story Elements Sections 1–5
Determine central ideas or themes of a text and analyze their development; summarize the key supporting details and ideas. (R.2)	Analyzing the Literature Sections 1–5; Guided Close Reading Sections 1–5; Making Connections Section 5; Post-Reading Response to Literature
Analyze how and why individuals, events, or ideas develop and interact over the course of a text. (R.3)	Analyzing the Literature Sections 1–5; Guided Close Reading Sections 1–5; Story Elements Sections 1–5; Making Connections Section 5; Post-Reading Response to Literature
Interpret words and phrases as they are used in a text, including determining technical, connotative, and figurative meanings, and analyze how specific word choices shape meaning or tone. (R.4)	Vocabulary Sections 1–5;
Write arguments to support claims in an analysis of substantive topics or texts using valid reasoning and relevant and sufficient evidence. (W.1)	Reader Response Sections 2, 4
Write informative/explanatory texts to examine and convey complex ideas and information clearly and accurately through the effective selection, organization, and analysis of content. (W.2)	Reader Response Section 5
Write narratives to develop real or imagined experiences or events using effective technique, well-chosen details and well-structured event sequences. (W.3)	Reader Response Sections 1, 3
Produce clear and coherent writing in which the development, organization, and style are appropriate to task, purpose, and audience. (W.4)	Reader Response Sections 1–5; Making Connections Section 4; Culminating Activity

correlation to the Standards (cont.)

Standards correlation chart (cont.)

College and Career Readiness Standard	Section
Demonstrate command of the conventions of standard English grammar and usage when writing or speaking. (L.1)	Reader Response Sections 1–5; Making Connections Section 4; Language Learning Sections 1–5; Story Elements Sections 1–5
Apply knowledge of language to understand how language functions in different contexts, to make effective choices for meaning or style, and to comprehend more fully when reading or listening. (L.3)	Analyzing the Literature Section 1–5; Guided Close Reading Sections 1–5; Language Learning Sections 2, 4, 5
Determine or clarify the meaning of unknown and multiple-meaning words and phrases by using context clues, analyzing meaningful word parts, and consulting general and specialized reference materials, as appropriate. (L.4)	Vocabulary Sections 1–5; Making Connections Section 2
Demonstrate understanding of figurative language, word relationships, and nuances in word meanings. (L.5)	Language Learning Section 4
Acquire and use accurately a range of general academic and domain-specific words and phrases sufficient for reading, writing, speaking, and listening at the college and career readiness level; demonstrate independence in gathering vocabulary knowledge when encountering an unknown term important to comprehension or expression. (L.6)	Vocabulary Sections 1–5; Making Connections Sections 2, 4; Story Elements Sections 1–5; Culminating Activity

TESOL and WIDA Standards

The lessons in this book promote English language development for English language learners. The following TESOL and WIDA English Language Development Standards are addressed through the activities in this book:

- **Standard 1:** English language learners communicate for social and instructional purposes within the school setting.

- **Standard 2:** English language learners communicate information, ideas and concepts necessary for academic success in the content area of language arts.

About the Author—Laura Numeroff

Laura Joffe Numeroff was born on July 14, 1953, in Brooklyn, New York. She grew up in a family where she was the youngest of three girls. Her family's house was busy with books, art, music, and folk dancing. Numeroff loved to read. She would check out the maximum amount of library books at a time and would lie on her bed and read for hours. At the young age of 9, she loved to write and tell stories and decided she would like to be a writer when she grew up.

Numeroff attended the Pratt Institute in Brookyln, New York, where she took classes in illustration, animation, and photography. She took a class titled Writing and Illustrating Children's Books. She wrote and illustrated the children's book *Amy for Short* for a homework assignment in that class. This homework assignment launched her writing career. In 1975, just before she graduated, Macmillan published the book.

If You Give a Mouse a Cookie was the tenth book she wrote. The idea came to her on a road trip from San Francisco to Oregon. She was trying to make a friend laugh by telling her a story about a mouse nibbling on a cookie. She had come up with the whole story by the time they reached Oregon. Nine publishers turned down *If You Give a Mouse a Cookie* before HarperCollins decided to publish it.

Numeroff's books have received numerous awards. At one point, she had three of her books on *The New York Times* Best Sellers list in the same week.

More information about Laura Numeroff and her books can be found at the following websites:

- http://www.lauranumeroff.com
- http://www.mousecookiebooks.com

Possible Texts for Text Comparisons

If You Take a Mouse to the Movies, *If You Take a Mouse to School*, and *If You Give a Pig a Party* are additional titles in the If You Give . . . series and could be used for enriching text comparisons by the same author. *What Mommies Do Best/What Daddies Do Best, Laura Numeroff's Ten Step Guide to Living with Your Monster* may also be used for engaging text comparisons.

Cross-Curricular Connection

These books can be used in a science unit on the circular pattern of the cycles of nature, such as the water cycle, animal life cycles, and seasonal cycles. They could also be used in a language arts unit on circular stories.

Book Summaries of the If You Give ... Series

If You Give a Mouse a Cookie—When a boy shares a cookie with a hungry mouse, the mouse asks for a glass of milk. The mouse continues to ask for many other things and keeps the boy busy all day long. The boy kindly grants all of the mouse's wishes. The boy eventually gives the mouse another cookie and the circle is complete.

If You Give a Moose a Muffin—This book is a sequel to *If You Give a Mouse a Cookie*. This time, the guest is a big moose that wanders in ready for a muffin with homemade blackberry jam. The story progresses with the boy cleaning up all the messes that the moose makes as he goes from one activity to another. The story comes full circle when the moose asks for another muffin.

If You Give a Cat a Cupcake—When a girl gives a cupcake to a cat, the cat wants some sprinkles for the cupcake. The cat continues to take the girl on a series of adventures where one thing leads to the next. Each event is triggered by a prior action or activity. At the end of these escapades, the cat is again reminded of the cupcakes and sprinkles, and we all know what happens when you give a cat a cupcake.

If You Give a Pig a Pancake—This story begins when a girl gives a pig a pancake. The pig then wants maple syrup to go with the pancake. After getting sticky from the syrup, the pig needs a bath, which leads to the pig asking for many other things. The girl gives the pig everything she asks for, eventually circling back to a pancake.

If You Give a Dog a Donut—This book follows the antics of a boy and a dog that is given a donut. The dog asks for some apple juice to go with the donut. Giving a dog a donut can lead to so much more. One thing leads to another until the boy gives the dog another donut, completing the circular story.

Possible Texts for Text Sets

- Frost, Hellen. *The Water Cycle*. Pebble Books, 2000.
- Gibbons, Gail. *The Reason for Seasons*. Holiday House, 1996.
- Himmelman, John. *A Ladybug's Life*. Children's Press, 1998.

or

- Eastman, P.D. *The Best Nest*. Random House, Inc., 1968.
- Hutchins, Pat. *Rosie's Walk*. Aladdin Paperbacks, 1971.
- McKee, David. *Elmer in the Snow*. Lothrop, Lee & Shepard Books, 1995.
- Stein, David Ezra. *Because Amelia Smiled*. Candlewick Press, 2012.

Pre-Reading Theme Thoughts

Directions: Read each statement. Draw a picture of a happy face or a sad face. The face should show how you feel about the statement. Then, use words to say why you feel this way.

Statement	How Do You Feel? 😊 ☹️	Explain Your Answer
One thing can lead to another.		
Be thankful for what you have.		
Treats lead to trouble!		
Working together is fun.		

Vocabulary Overview

Key words and phrases from this book are provided below with definitions and sentences about how the words are used in the story. Introduce and discuss these important vocabulary words with students. If you think these words or other words in the story warrant more time devoted to them, there are suggestions in the introduction for other vocabulary activities (page 5).

Word or Phrase	Definition	Sentence about Text
probably	very likely; almost certainly	The mouse will **probably** ask for a straw.
mustache	hair on the upper lip	The mouse looks to see if he has a milk **mustache**.
notice	to become aware of by seeing or hearing	The mouse **notices** his hair needs a trim.
trim	an act of making something neat by cutting it	The mouse wants to **trim** his hair.
pair	a thing that has two parts that are joined	The mouse asks for a **pair** of nail scissors.
sweep	to remove something from a surface with a broom or brush	The mouse wants to **sweep** up.
carried away	to be so excited that you are no longer in control of your behavior	The mouse gets **carried away**.
comfortable	not having any physically unpleasant feelings	The mouse makes himself **comfortable**.
fluff	to shake or move something so that it is fuller, lighter, or softer	The mouse **fluffs** the pillow.
excited	very enthusiastic and eager about something	The pictures make the mouse **excited**.

Name _____

Vocabulary Activity

Directions: These sentences describe *If You Give a Mouse a Cookie.* Cut apart the sentence strips. Put them in order. Use the story to help you.

The mouse gets **excited**, and he wants to draw.

The mouse **notices** his hair needs a trim.

The mouse uses a broom to **sweep** up.

The mouse looks to see if he has a milk **mustache**.

The mouse **fluffs** his pillow before he takes a nap.

Analyzing the Literature

Provided below are discussion questions you can use in small groups, with the whole class, or for written assignments. Each question is written at two levels so you can choose the right question for each group of students. For each question, a few key points are provided for your reference as you discuss the book with students.

Story Element	Level 1	Level 2	Key Discussion Points
Character	Who are the characters in the story?	Describe how each character is introduced in the story.	The characters are a mouse and a boy. They are both introduced on the first two pages of the story. The boy is shown sitting on a rock in his front lawn and leaning over to give the mouse a cookie.
Setting	Where does most of the story take place?	Describe the different settings in the story.	The story begins outside of the boy's house, but most of the story takes place in various rooms inside the house. The boy and the mouse are mainly in the kitchen, the bathroom, and the hallway.
Plot	Why does the mouse need a broom?	Describe the actions leading up to the mouse needing a broom.	The mouse needs a broom because he gives himself a trim with nail scissors. The mouse notices he needs a trim when he looks at himself in the mirror to see if he has a milk mustache. He uses the broom to sweep up the hair.
Character	How does the boy feel at the end of the story?	Describe how the boy feels at the end of the story and why he feels that way.	Based on the illustrations, the boy looks tired. Towards the end of the book, the illustrations show the boy sitting in the chair and sitting on the floor looking exhausted. The mouse has kept him very busy with all of his requests.

Name _____

Reader Response

Think

Think about a time you have made cookies with someone.

Narrative Writing Prompt

Write about a time you made cookies with someone. Write about what kind of cookies you made, how they tasted, and who you made them with.

_____
_____
_____
_____
_____
_____
_____
_____
_____
_____
_____

Name _____

Guided Close Reading

Closely reread where the boy makes a bed for the mouse and reads the mouse a story.

Directions: Think about these questions. In the space below, write ideas or draw pictures as you think. Be ready to share your answers.

❶ Look at the book. How does the boy make the mouse a bed?

❷ Use the text to find what the mouse asks to see.

❸ Use the book to tell what makes the mouse excited.

Making connections—counting chips

Directions: The cookies below are missing their chocolate chips! Look at the numbers connected to the cookies. The numbers tell you how many chocolate chips should be on the cookies. Draw the right number of chocolate chips on each cookie.

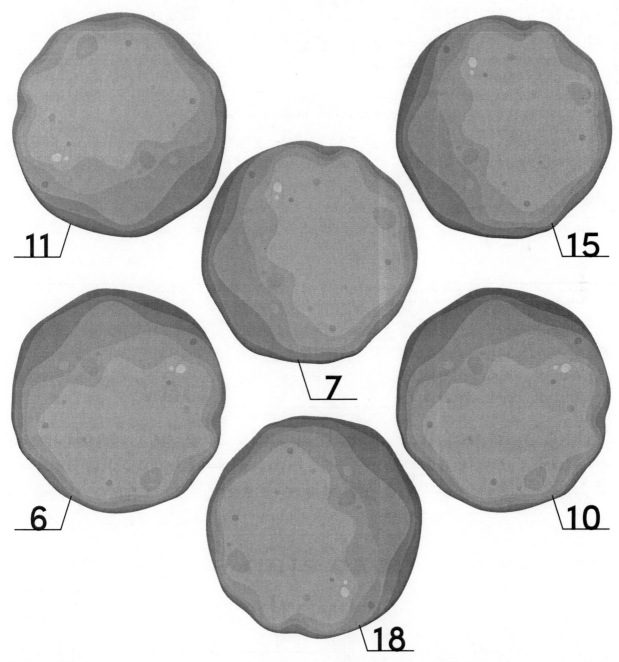

11

15

7

6

10

18

Name _____

Language Learning—Vowels

Directions: Some of these words are in *If You Give a Mouse a Cookie*. Sort the words into the correct columns. **Hint:** Look carefully at the vowels.

Word Bank

mouse	broom	box	out	room
house	hot	top	looks	

ou   **oo**   **o**

_____   _____   _____

- - - - - - - - -   - - - - - - - - -   - - - - - - - - -

_____   _____   _____

_____   _____   _____

- - - - - - - - -   - - - - - - - - -   - - - - - - - - -

_____   _____   _____

_____   _____   _____

- - - - - - - - -   - - - - - - - - -   - - - - - - - - -

_____   _____   _____

If You Give a Mouse a Cookie

Story Elements—character

Directions: Write an acrostic poem to describe the mouse. Each line should start with the big letter on the left.

M _____

O _____

U _____

S _____

E _____

Name _____

Story Elements—Plot

Directions: This story is made up of many cause-and-effect situations. Look at the causes below. Then, write or draw a picture of each effect.

Cause	Effect
The mouse has some milk.	
The mouse looks in the mirror.	
The mouse washes the floor.	
The mouse looks at the pictures in the book.	

Vocabulary Overview

Key words and phrases from this book are provided below with definitions and sentences about how the words are used in the story. Introduce and discuss these important vocabulary words with students. If you think these words or other words in the story warrant more time devoted to them, there are suggestions in the introduction for other vocabulary activities (page 5).

Word	Definition	Sentence about Text
chilly	noticeably cold	The moose feels how **chilly** it is.
borrow	to take and use something for a period of time before returning it	The moose asks to **borrow** a sweater.
notice	to become aware of something or someone by seeing or hearing	The moose **notices** one of the buttons is loose.
loose	not tightly fastened, attached, or held	One of the sweater's buttons is **loose**.
thread	a long, thin strand used for sewing	The moose asks for **thread**.
cardboard	a stiff and thick kind of paper used for making boxes	The moose needs some **cardboard** and paint to make the scenery.
scenery	the background during a performance that shows the setting	The moose wants to make **scenery** for his puppet show.
antlers	the horns of an animal	The moose's **antlers** stick out.
sheet	a large piece of thin cloth used on a bed	The boy brings the moose a **sheet** from his bed.
clothesline	a piece of rope that people hang wet clothes on to dry	The moose goes outside to put the sheet on the **clothesline**.

Name _____

Vocabulary Activity

Directions: Choose at least two words from the story. Draw a picture that shows what the words mean. Label your picture.

Words from the Story

chilly	borrow	notice	loose	thread
cardboard	scenery	antlers	sheet	clothesline

Directions: Answer this question.

1. Why does the moose need a needle and **thread**?

_____

_ _

_____

Analyzing the Literature

Provided below are discussion questions you can use in small groups, with the whole class, or for written assignments. Each question is written at two levels so you can choose the right question for each group of students. For each question, a few key points are provided for your reference as you discuss the book with students.

Story Element	Level 1	Level 2	Key Discussion Points
Setting	Describe the setting shown in the illustrations.	Describe the details that show the season in which the story takes place.	The setting begins in front of the boy's home and continues inside the house, including the kitchen and the living room. It looks as though it is fall because of the leaves on the ground, the bare limbs of the trees, and the fact that Halloween is mentioned.
Character	Who are the characters in the story?	Describe how each character is introduced in the story.	The moose is introduced visually on the first page. The narrator tells about the moose's actions beginning on the second page. The boy is introduced on the second page. The mother is mentioned and shown on a few pages later in the story.
Plot	What kind of show do the moose and the boy want to put on?	Describe how the moose and the boy prepare for the puppet show.	The moose wants to put on a puppet show. He makes sock puppets. They use cardboard and different paints to create the scenery.
Plot	What do the moose and the boy do with the sheet?	Describe how the sheet plays a role in the story.	The moose tries the sheet on and pretends to be a ghost. He shouts, "BOO!" He uses the sheet to clean up the paints that spilled. They wash the sheet with soap and then look for a clothesline on which to hang the sheet to dry.

Name _____

Reader Response

Think about the moose. Should the boy have given the moose a muffin?

Opinion Writing Prompt

Write about whether or not you think the boy should have given the moose a muffin. Tell why or why not. Include reasons for your opinion.

_____

_____

_____

_____

_____

_____

_____

_____

_____

_____

_____

Guided Close Reading

Closely reread the part of the book where the moose wants to go to the store with the boy.

Directions: Think about these questions. In the space below, write ideas or draw pictures as you think. Be ready to share your answers.

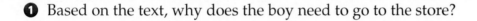

❶ Based on the text, why does the boy need to go to the store?

❷ Use the text to find out what the moose wants because it is chilly.

❸ What is the moose doing when he notices the loose button?

Name _____

Making Connections—Fact or Opinion?

Directions: Each sentence below is either a true fact or an opinion. A fact is a statement that can be proven. An opinion is a belief that cannot be proven. Read each sentence below. If the sentence is a fact, write the letter *F*. If the sentence is an opinion, write the letter *O*.

_____
_ _ _ _ _

1. Moose only eat plants. _____

_____
_ _ _ _ _

2. Moose are the most beautiful animals. _____

_____
_ _ _ _ _

3. Moose can swim. _____

_____
_ _ _ _ _

4. Moose have 32 teeth. _____

_____
_ _ _ _ _

5. Moose are not nice. _____

_____
_ _ _ _ _

6. Moose have a good sense of smell. _____

Language Learning— contraction Match Up

Directions: Below are contractions used in *If You Give a Moose a Muffin.* A contraction is a word that uses an apostrophe to replace one or more missing letters. Match each contraction to the two words that it is based on.

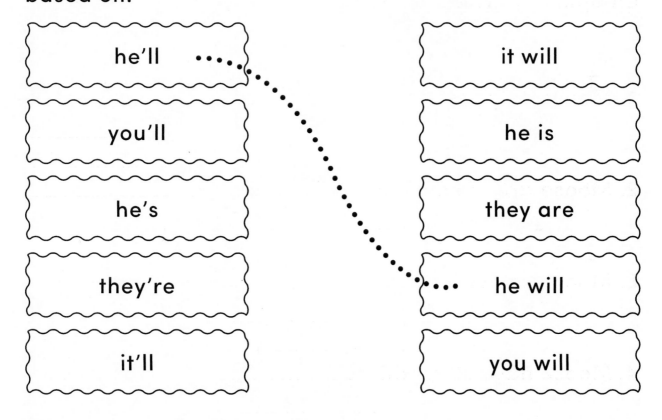

he'll	it will
you'll	he is
he's	they are
they're	he will
it'll	you will

Directions: Use one of these contractions in a sentence.

_____

_____

_____

_____

Name _____

Story Elements—Setting

Directions: Draw your favorite setting from the book. Include things that you can see, smell, hear, taste, and touch. Write a sentence about your picture.

_____

_____

_____

_____

Story Elements—Plot

Directions: Draw four things that the moose makes a mess of in the story. Label each of your pictures.

Vocabulary Overview

Key words and phrases from this book are provided below with definitions and sentences about how the words are used in the story. Introduce and discuss these important vocabulary words with students. If you think these words or other words in the story warrant more time devoted to them, there are suggestions in the introduction for other vocabulary activities (page 5).

Word	Definition	Sentence about Text
sprinkles	tiny candies that are put on top of sweet food	The cat wants **sprinkles** on the cupcake.
beach	an area covered with sand or small rocks that is next to an ocean or lake	The girl takes the cat to the **beach**.
seashells	the hard, empty shell of small sea creatures	The cat looks for **seashells**.
pail	a round container that is open at the top and usually has a handle	The cat puts many things in his **pail**.
treadmill	an exercise machine that has a large belt that moves around for a person to walk or run on	The cat will warm up on the **treadmill**.
karate	a form of fighting where you hit and kick an opponent with your hands and feet	The cat might try a **karate** class.
rowing	moving a boat by using oars	The cat wants to go **rowing** on the lake.
captain	a person in charge of a boat, ship, or airplane	The cat is the **captain** of the boat.
mane	long, thick hair growing from the neck of an animal, specifically a horse or a lion	The horse has a purple **mane**.
whale	a large mammal that lives in the ocean	The **whale** reminds the cat of the science museum.

Vocabulary Activity

Directions: Complete each sentence below. Use one of the words from the box.

Words from the Story

sprinkles	beach	seashells	pail	treadmill
karate	rowing	captain	mane	whale

1. The cat looks for _____ at

   the _____.

2. He might spill _____ on the floor.

3. The cat tries a _____ class.

4. He wants to go _____ on the lake.

Directions: Answer this question.

5. What does the cat put in the **pail**?

_____

_____

_____

_____

Analyzing the Literature

Provided below are discussion questions you can use in small groups, with the whole class, or for written assignments. Each question is written at two levels so you can choose the right question for each group of students. For each question, a few key points are provided for your reference as you discuss the book with students.

Story Element	Level 1	Level 2	Key Discussion Points
Plot	Why do the girl and the cat go to the beach?	What things do the girl and the cat do at the beach?	The girl and the cat are hot, so they go to the beach. They go in the water. They build a sand castle and look for seashells. The cat finds many other things and puts them in his pail.
Setting	List three of the places where the cat goes.	Describe the places or different settings that the cat goes to in this story.	First, the cat is in the kitchen. The cat and the girl then go to the beach and play in the water and the sand. Next, they go to the gym. Then, they go to a lake and go rowing. They both go for a ride on a merry-go-round. Then, they go to the science museum. Lastly, they head back home.
Character	Why does the cat think he needs to work out at the gym?	What leads up to the idea that the cat needs to work out at the gym?	The cat puts many things in his pail at the beach. He tries to pick it up, but it is too heavy. The cat decides that he needs to work out at the gym because he is unable to lift the heavy pail.
Character	Which character is your favorite?	If you could be any character in the story, which character would you choose? Why?	Students should share their favorite character and give supporting reasons.

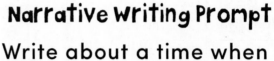

If You Give a cat a cupcake

Reader Response

Think

The cat goes to the beach and to a lake. Think of a time when you have gone to a beach or a lake.

Narrative Writing Prompt

Write about a time when you went to a beach or to a lake. Describe what you did there and who you went with.

_____

- - - - - - - - - - - - - - - - - - -

_____

- - - - - - - - - - - - - - - - - - -

_____

- - - - - - - - - - - - - - - - - - -

_____

- - - - - - - - - - - - - - - - - - -

_____

- - - - - - - - - - - - - - - - - - -

_____

- - - - - - - - - - - - - - - - - - -

_____

Name _____

Guided Close Reading

Closely reread where the cat climbs up on the rocks and then visits the lake with the girl.

Directions: Think about these questions. In the space below, write ideas or draw pictures as you think. Be ready to share your answers.

❶ What words tell you where the cat was before going to the park?

❷ Use the book to describe how the cat sees the lake.

❸ Look at the text and illustrations to tell who has to do the rowing.

Name _____

Making Connections—Exercise

Directions: The cat exercises in the story. Exercise is very important to keep our bodies healthy. Draw two exercises that the cat does. Then, draw two activities you do to exercise. Be sure to label your pictures.

Exercises the Cat Does

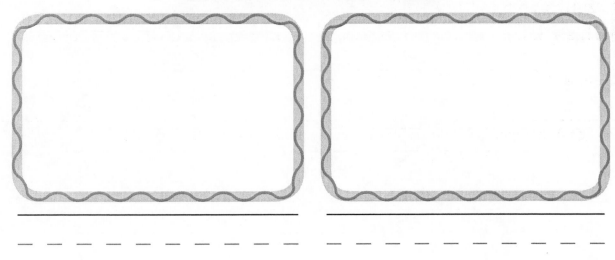

Exercises I Do

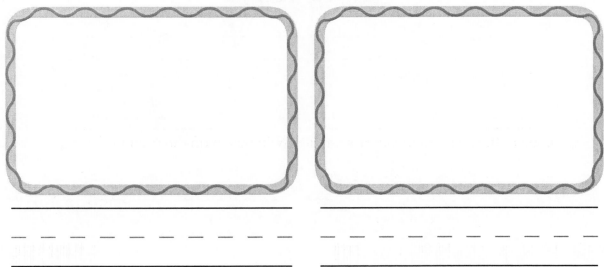

Name _____

Language Learning—Animals in Order

Directions: There are many animals seen throughout *If You Give a Cat a Cupcake*. Rewrite the list of animals below in alphabetical order.

- cat
- horse
- whale
- dinosaur
- apes
- mouse

1. _____

2. _____

3. _____

4. _____

5. _____

6. _____

Name _____

Story Elements—Plot

Directions: Cut apart the strips. Then, glue them in the order of the story on another piece of paper.

The cat builds a sand castle.

The cat sees dinosaurs at the science museum.

The cat goes on a merry-go-round ride.

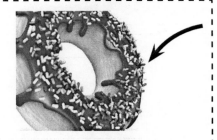

The cat spills some sprinkles on the floor.

The cat tries a karate class.

Name _____

Story Elements—Character

Directions: Draw a picture of the cat. Write descriptive words around the cat. Be sure to use many strong words to tell about the cat.

Vocabulary Overview

Key words and phrases from this book are provided below with definitions and sentences about how the words are used in the story. Introduce and discuss these important vocabulary words with students. If you think these words or other words in the story warrant more time devoted to them, there are suggestions in the introduction for other vocabulary activities (page 5).

Word or Phrase	Definition	Sentence about Text
maple syrup	a sweet, thick liquid made from the sap of maple trees	The girl gives the pig some **maple syrup**.
sticky	covered in a substance that things adhere to	The pig is **sticky** from the syrup.
homesick	sad because you are away from your family and home	The pig feels **homesick**.
suitcase	a large container used to carry things when you travel	The pig looks through the closet for a **suitcase**.
tap shoes	shoes with metal plates on the toes and heels	The pig finds **tap shoes** under the bed.
envelopes	paper covers for letters or cards	The girl gives the pig some **envelopes** and stamps.
stamps	small pieces of paper that are stuck to envelopes or packages to pay for postage	The girl helps the pig put the **stamps** on the envelopes.
hammer	a tool that has a metal head attached to a handle and is used for hitting nails	The girl gives the pig some wood, a **hammer**, and some nails.
decorate	to make something more attractive usually by putting something on it	The pig wants to **decorate** the tree house.
wallpaper	thick decorative paper used to cover the walls of a room	The pig asks for some **wallpaper** and glue.

Name _____

Vocabulary Activity

Directions: Draw lines to complete the sentences.

Beginnings of Sentences	Endings of Sentences
She'll want to	give her **wallpaper** and glue.
To decorate the treehouse, you'll	**decorate** the treehouse.
She'll look through	some of your favorite **maple syrup**.
She'll ask for	your closet for a **suitcase**.

Directions: Answer this question.

1. Where does the pig find old **tap shoes**?

_____

_ _ _ _ _ _ _ _ _ _ _ _ _ _ _ _ _

_____

Analyzing the Literature

Provided below are discussion questions you can use in small groups, with the whole class, or for written assignments. Each question is written at two levels so that you can choose the right question for each group of students. For each question, a few key points are provided for your reference as you discuss the book with students.

Story Element	Level 1	Level 2	Key Discussion Points
Setting	Where does the story mainly take place?	How do the illustrations show the setting of this story?	This story mainly takes place inside and outside of the girl's house. The illustrations show the pig and the girl in the kitchen, upstairs in the bathroom, and in the girl's room. Then, they come back downstairs to the living room. Finally, they end up outside working on the tree house.
Character	Based on the illustrations, how does the girl feel at the very end of the story?	Look at the illustrations and describe how the girl's mood changes from the beginning of the story to the end.	In the beginning of the story, the girl looks very happy to give the pig a pancake. She looks like she is having fun as they go to the different places. By the end of the story, the girl looks tired. On the last page, the girl has her head down on the table.
Plot	What does the pig want in the bath?	Describe the bath that the pig takes.	The pig wants bubbles in the bath. She also asks for a toy. The girl finds a rubber duck for the pig.
Plot	What is the most exciting part of this story?	Describe the most exciting part of the story and why it is exciting to you.	Students should describe with details the parts of the story that are most exciting to them.

Name _____

Reader Response

Think

The pig builds a tree house. She wants to decorate it. Think about how the pig should decorate the tree house.

Opinion Writing Prompt

Write about how you think the pig should decorate the tree house. Give the pig some ideas for decorating the tree house.

_____

- - - - - - - - - - - - - - - - -

_____

- - - - - - - - - - - - - - - - -

_____

- - - - - - - - - - - - - - - - -

_____

- - - - - - - - - - - - - - - - -

_____

- - - - - - - - - - - - - - - - -

_____

- - - - - - - - - - - - - - - - -

_____

Name _____

Guided close Reading

Closely reread the part of the story where the pig takes a bath.

Directions: Think about these questions. In the space below, write ideas or draw pictures as you think. Be ready to share your answers.

❶ Use the images to describe how the pig feels as she gets ready.

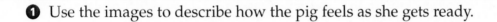

❷ What does the rubber duck reminds the pig of?

❸ Describe the pig when she is thinking about the farm where she was born.

Name _____

Making connections—Writing Letters

Directions: The girl takes pictures of the pig. Then, the pig sends the pictures to her friends. Draw a picture to send to one of your friends. Then, write your friend a short letter.

_____

Dear _____ ,

_____

_____

_____

_____

_____

_____

_____

From , _____

Language Learning—compound Words

Directions: The words below are compound words from *If You Give a Pig a Pancake*. A compound word is a word that is made up of two words with its own new meaning. Read the compound words below. Then, write the two words that make up each compound word.

suitcase = _____ + _____

mailbox = _____ + _____

pancake = _____ + _____

homesick = _____ + _____

backyard = _____ + _____

wallpaper = _____ + _____

Name _____

Story Elements—Plot

Directions: Sketch four main events from the story in order on this chart.

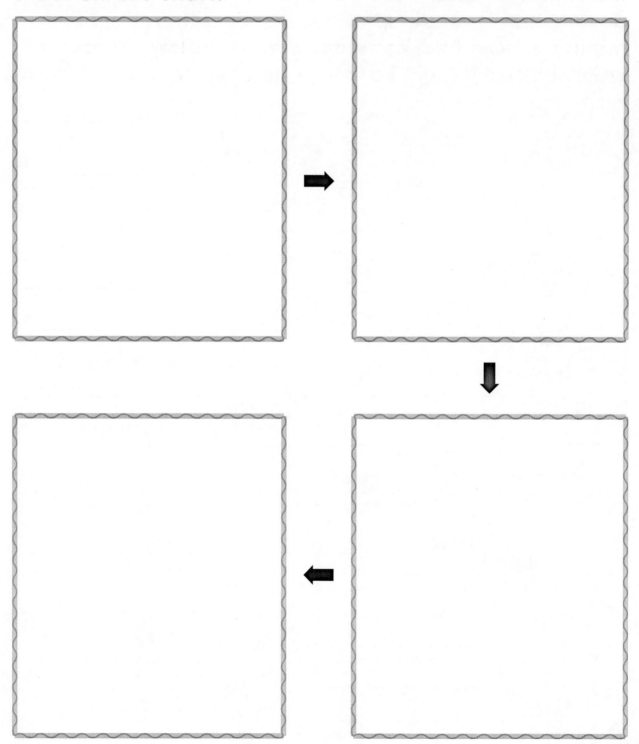

 #40012—Instructional Guide: If You Give . . . Series Guide

Story Elements—character

Directions: The girl feels many different emotions in the story. Look closely at the illustrations in the book. Draw pictures of two different emotions she might be feeling. Write a sentence to describe each of your pictures.

Vocabulary Overview

Key words and phrases from this book are provided below with definitions and sentences about how the words are used in the story. Introduce and discuss these important vocabulary words with students. If you think these words or other words in the story warrant more time devoted to them, there are suggestions in the introduction for other vocabulary activities (pages 5).

Word or Phrase	Definition	Sentence about Text
pick	to remove a fruit or flower from a plant	The dog goes outside to **pick** apples.
toss	to throw something with a quick, light motion	The dog **tosses** the boy an apple.
glove	a leather cover for the hand used to catch a ball	The boy has to get a **glove**.
pitch	to throw a baseball to a batter	The dog asks the boy to **pitch**.
home run	a hit that allows the batter to go around all the bases and score a run	The dog hits a **home run**!
celebrate	to do something special or enjoyable for an important event, occasion, or holiday	The dog does a happy dance to **celebrate**.
dusty	covered with dry dirt or sand	The dog is hot and **dusty**.
bandanna	a square piece of cloth that is used as a head covering or worn around the neck	The boy dries off the dog with his **bandanna**.
string	a long, thin piece of twisted thread that is used to attach, tie, or hang things	The boy gets some **string** for the kite.
tangled	became twisted together	The kite is **tangled** in the tree.

Name _____

Vocabulary Activity

Directions: Practice your writing skills. Write at least two sentences using words from the story.

Words from the Story

pick	toss	glove	pitch	home run
celebrate	dusty	bandanna	string	tangled

_____

- -

_____

- -

_____

- -

_____

- -

_____

Directions: Answer this question.

1. Why does the dog need the **bandanna**?

_____

- -

_____

- -

_____

Analyzing the Literature

Provided below are discussion questions you can use in small groups, with the whole class, or for written assignments. Each question is written at two levels so you can choose the right question for each group of students. For each question, a few key points are provided for your reference as you discuss the book with students.

Story Element	Level 1	Level 2	Key Discussion Points
Setting	Describe the setting of the story.	Describe how the setting changes throughout the story.	The story begins with the dog outside of the house with his dog bowl. The story then moves inside the house with the boy giving the dog a donut. The illustrations show the kitchen and a hallway. The boy and the dog then go outside. They have fun outside with the apple tree, fountain, kite, and on a treasure hunt.
Plot	What does the dog do with the bandanna?	Describe why the dog needs a bandanna. What does the dog do with it?	The boy uses the bandanna to dry the dog off when he gets wet from the water fight. The dog then wraps the bandanna around his head and pretends that he's a pirate.
Plot	What materials are used to make the kite?	How might the kite be made and what do the boy and dog do with it when they are finished.	The boy gets some sticks, comic paper, and string. The tail of the kite has the bandanna attached at the very bottom. They fly the kite high in the sky until it gets tangled in the apple tree.
Character	Do you think the dog belongs to the boy?	Give reasons as to why you do or do not think the dog belongs to the boy.	Unlike some of the other stories with a moose or a pig, the dog is likely to be the boy's pet. There are pictures of the dog in frames hanging on the wall in the kitchen, which makes it seem as though the dog may belong to the boy.

Reader Response

Think

The dog and the boy try to fly a kite. Think about the steps it takes to fly a kite.

Informative/Explanatory Writing Prompt

Write all the steps it takes to fly a kite. Be sure to be specific.

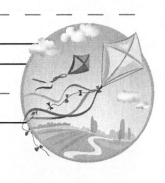

Name _____

Guided close Reading

Closely reread the part where the dog celebrates and plays in the water fountain.

Directions: Think about these questions. In the space below, write ideas or draw pictures as you think. Be ready to share your answers.

❶ How does the dog celebrate? Look at the text and images.

❷ Based on the events in the book, why does the dog need some water?

❸ Based on the pictures, how does the dog get dry?

Making connections—circle stories

Directions: This story is a circle story. Cut out the pictures on page 56. Put them in the correct order.

Making connections— circle stories *(cont.)*

Directions: Cut apart the pictures below. Glue them in the correct order on page 55.

Name _____

Language Learning—Nouns and Verbs

Directions: Nouns are words that name people, places, and things. Verbs are action words that show what is happening. Read the words from the story at the bottom of the page. Cut apart the words. Decide if each word is a noun or a verb in the story, and glue it in the correct column.

Nouns—Naming Words	Verbs—Action Words

juice	drink	dog	donut	hit	fly	throw	kite

Name _____

Story Elements—Setting

Directions: Draw two different settings from the story. Only include details from the illustrations or text. Label each of your pictures.

Story Elements—Plot

Directions: The events in a story are part of the plot. Match each sequence word with the correct event from this story.

First	The dog will go outside to pick apples.
Next	The dog will fly a kite.
Lastly	The dog will ask for some juice.

Name _____

Post-Reading Theme Thoughts

Directions: Choose a main character from one of the If You Give . . . stories. Pretend you are that character. Draw a picture of a happy face or a sad face to show how the character would feel about each statement. Then, use words to explain your picture.

Character I Chose: _____

Statement	How Do You Feel? ☺ ☹	Explain Your Answer
One thing can lead to another.		
Be thankful for what you have.		
Treats lead to trouble!		
Working together is fun.		

Culminating Activity: Stick Puppets and Reader's Theater

Directions: Work with students to help them choose one of the following activities. Most likely, these activities will require adult assistance to complete. Reproduce the stick puppet patterns on pages 61–62 on tagboard or construction paper. Have students cut the puppets along the dashed lines. To complete the stick puppets, glue each pattern to a tongue depressor or craft stick. The stick puppets may be fun for the students to use as they perform these different activities.

- Write and illustrate your own If You Give . . . story. Be sure to make a circle story. Try to title your story with alliteration. For example, you could write *If You Give a Turtle a Taco*, *If You Give a Rabbit Some Rice*, or *If You Take a Butterfly to the Beach*. You could make your own sock puppets or stick puppets for your characters.

- Prepare the stick puppets to use with the reader's theater script on pages 63–64. Let pairs of students take turns reading the parts and using the stick puppets.

- Practice retelling the different stories. You could use the stick puppets from pages 61–62 to retell *If You Give a Pig a Pancake*. You could make your own sock puppets or stick puppets for the different characters in the other stories.

culminating Activity: Stick Puppets and Reader's Theater (cont.)

If You Take a Pig to the Park

Characters

- Girl
- Pig

Girl: If you take a pig to the park, she'll ask you to push her on the swings.

Pig: When I am being pushed on the swings, I'll feel like I am flying.

Girl: She'll probably ask you to take her to the airport.

Pig: At the airport, I'll want to watch the planes.

Girl: Watching the planes will give her the idea to make her own plane. You'll have to get paper and scissors.

Pig: When I am finished making my plane, I'll want to fly it in your backyard.

Girl: When she launches the plane in the air, it will crash into your sandbox.

Pig: When I see the sandbox, I'll want to play in it.

Girl: She'll probably make sand pies.

Pig: Sand pies will remind me of real pie, and I'll want to make one.

If You Take a Pig to the Park (cont.)

Girl: When she is done making the pie, you'll have to clean up the kitchen with a mop.

Pig: After cleaning up, I'll want to eat the pie.

Girl: She'll get pie all over her face, and she'll ask for a washcloth to wipe off the crumbs.

Pig: When I look in the mirror, I'll notice I need a haircut.

Girl: She'll ask you to take her to the hair salon.

Pig: Once I get my haircut, I'll get a lollipop.

Girl: She'll want to enjoy her lollipop in your backyard.

Pig: When I am done, I'll want to play a game of tag.

Girl: She'll run around and tag you! While she's chasing you, she'll notice the swings.

Pig: I will want to be pushed on the swings.

Girl: And chances are, if you push her on the swings, she'll want to go to the park again.

comprehension Assessment

Directions: Fill in the bubble for the best response to each question.

If You Give a Mouse a Cookie

1. After the mouse washes the floors, what does he want to do?

    Ⓐ draw a picture

    Ⓑ eat a cookie

    Ⓒ sweep the floor

    Ⓓ take a nap

If You Give a Moose a Muffin

2. Why does the boy have to go to the store?

    Ⓐ to borrow a sweater

    Ⓑ to get some muffin mix

    Ⓒ to buy some paints

    Ⓓ to get some jam

If You Give a cat a cupcake

3. Describe what the girl and the cat do at the beach.

_____

_____

_____

_____

_____

_____

comprehension Assessment (cont.)

If You Give a Pig a Pancake

4. What does the pig ask for after she is all dressed?

(A) for some music

(B) for some syrup

(C) for wallpaper

(D) for some wood, a hammer, and some nails

If You Give a Dog a Donut

5. What does throwing the apple remind the dog of?

(A) dancing

(B) a donut

(C) baseball

(D) a water fight

Response to Literature:
Cause and Effect

Directions: All of the If You Give . . . stories are based on cause and effect. A cause is an action or an event. The effect is what happens because of that action or event. Draw a picture of your favorite scene from one of the If You Give . . . stories. Then, draw a picture of the effect of that scene. Make sure your pictures are neat and colorful.

Cause

Effect

Response to Literature: Cause and Effect (cont.)

1. Why is this your favorite scene?

   _____

   _____

   _____

   _____

   _____

2. Why does the effect happen?

   _____

   _____

   _____

   _____

   _____

3. What happens next in the story?

   _____

   _____

   _____

   _____

   _____

Name _____

Response to Literature Rubric

Directions: Use this rubric to evaluate student responses.

Great Job	Good Work	Keep Trying
☐ You answered all three questions completely. You included many details.	☐ You answered all three questions.	☐ You did not answer all three questions.
☐ Your handwriting is very neat. There are no spelling errors.	☐ Your handwriting can be neater. There are some spelling errors.	☐ Your handwriting is not very neat. There are many spelling errors.
☐ Your picture is neat and fully colored.	☐ Your picture is neat and some of it is colored.	☐ Your picture is not very neat and/or fully colored.
☐ Creativity is clear in both the picture and the writing.	☐ Creativity is clear in either the picture or the writing.	☐ There is not much creativity in either the picture or the writing.

Teacher Comments: _____

_____

_____

_____

Name _____

The responses provided here are just examples of what students may answer. Many accurate responses are possible for the questions throughout this unit.

Vocabulary Activity—Section 1:
If You Give a Mouse a Cookie (page 15)
The following sentences should be placed in this order.

- The mouse looks to see if he has a milk **mustache**.
- The mouse **notices** his hair needs a trim.
- The mouse uses a broom to **sweep** up.
- The mouse **fluffs** his pillow before he takes a nap.
- The mouse gets **excited**, and he wants to draw.

Guided Close Reading—Section 1:
If You Give a Mouse a Cookie (page 18)

1. The boy fixes up a little box with a blanket and a pillow. The box is a powder box. The blanket is a bandanna, and the pillow is a powder puff.
2. The mouse asks to see the pictures in the story.
3. The pictures in the book make the mouse excited to draw a picture.

Making Connections—Section 1:
If You Give a Mouse a Cookie (page 19)
The numbers of chocolate chips drawn should match the numbers below the cookies.

Language Learning—Section 1:
If You Give a Mouse a Cookie (page 20)

ou	oo	o
mouse	broom	box
house	room	hot
out	looks	top

Story Elements—Section 1:
If You Give a Mouse a Cookie (page 22)

Cause	Effect
The mouse has some milk.	He'll ask for a straw
The mouse looks in the mirror.	He notices his hair needs a trim.
The mouse washes the floor.	He'll want to take a nap.
The mouse looks at the pictures in the book.	He'll want to draw his own picture.

Vocabulary Activity—Section 2:
If You Give a Moose a Muffin (page 24)
Students' drawings will vary.

1. The moose needs a needle and **thread** to sew a loose button on the sweater.

Guided Close Reading—Section 2:
If You Give a Moose a Muffin (page 27)

1. The boy needs to go to the store to buy more muffin mix.
2. The moose wants to borrow a sweater.
3. The moose is putting on a sweater when he notices that a button is loose.

Making Connections—Section 2:
If You Give a Moose a Muffin (page 28)

1. F
2. O
3. F
4. F
5. O
6. F

Language Learning—Section 2:
If You Give a Moose a Muffin (page 29)

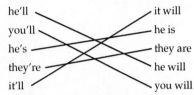

he'll	it will
you'll	he is
he's	they are
they're	he will
it'll	you will

1. Students' sentences will vary but should use one of the contractions.

Story Elements—Section 2:
If You Give a Moose a Muffin (page 30)
Students' drawings will vary but should include a drawing of a setting that shows many details.

Story Elements—Section 2:
If You Give a Moose a Muffin (page 31)
Students' drawings will vary but should include four different messes the moose makes: spilling the vase, cutting up socks to make puppets, cardboard and paint all over the living room, and dripping a wet sheet in the house. The pictures should be labeled.

Vocabulary Activity—Section 3:
If You Give a Cat a Cupcake (page 33)

1. The cat looks for **seashells** at the **beach**.
2. He might spill **sprinkles** on the floor.
3. The cat tries a **karate** class.
4. He wants to go **rowing** on the lake.
5. Students' responses will vary but might include the following things that were put in the pail: seashells, glasses, an umbrella, a kite, an airplane, a ball, a surfboard, or a toy truck.

Guided Close Reading—Section 3:
If You Give a Cat a Cupcake (page 36)

1. "After the gym" shows that the cat worked out before going to the park.
2. The cat climbs the rocks and sees the lake when he is at top.
3. The girl has to do the rowing.

Making Connections—Section 3:
If You Give a Cat a Cupcake (page 37)
Students' drawings will vary but might include swimming, going on the treadmill, lifting weights, karate, and rowing. The drawings should be labeled.

Answer Key

Language Learning—Section 3:
If You Give a Cat a Cupcake (page 38)

1. apes
2. cat
3. dinosaur
4. horse
5. mouse
6. whale

Story Elements—Section 3:
If You Give a Cat a Cupcake (page 39)
The order of the cards should be as follows:

- The cat spills some sprinkles on the floor.
- The cat builds a sand castle.
- The cat tries a karate class.
- The cat goes on a merry-go-round ride.
- The cat sees dinosaurs at the museum.

Story Elements—Section 3:
If You Give a Cat a Cupcake (page 40)
Students should have descriptive words written around the cat.

Vocabulary Activity—Section 4:
If You Give a Pig a Pancake (page 42)
Sentences should be completed as follows:

- She'll want to **decorate** the treehouse.
- To decorate the treehouse, you'll give her **wallpaper** and glue.
- She'll look through your closet for a **suitcase**.
- She'll ask for some of your favorite **maple syrup**.

1. The pig finds old **tap shoes** under the bed.

Guided Close Reading—Section 4:
If You Give a Pig a Pancake (page 45)

1. The pig is jumping and happy. The pictures show a smile on her face.
2. The rubber duck reminds the pig of the farm where she was born.
3. Her face looks sad and thoughtful. She is holding the rubber duck.

Language Learning—Section 4:
If You Give a Pig a Pancake (page 47)

- **suitcase** suit case
- **mailbox** mail box
- **pancake** pan cake
- **homesick** home sick
- **backyard** back yard
- **wallpaper** wall paper

Story Elements—Section 4:
If You Give a Pig a Pancake (page 48)
Students' four main events will vary, but they should be in the correct order.

Story Elements—Section 4:
If You Give a Pig a Pancake (page 49)
Students' drawings will vary but should include a sentence describing the two different feelings of the girl.

Vocabulary Activity—Section 5:
If You Give a Dog a Donut (page 51)
Students' sentences will vary but should include the words in the word bank.

1. The dog needs the **bandanna** to dry himself off after the water fight.

Guided Close Reading—Section 5:
If You Give a Dog a Donut (page 54)

1. The dog celebrates by dancing.
2. The dog needs water because he is hot and dusty from dancing.
3. The dog gets dry when the boy dries him off using the bandanna.

Making Connections—Section 5:
If You Give a Dog a Donut (page 55)
Students should glue the pictures in the following order: gets a donut, drinks juice, picks apples, plays baseball, plays in water, hunts for treasure, and flies a kite.

Language Learning—Section 5:
If You Give a Dog a Donut (page 57)

nouns	verbs
juice	drink
dog	hit
donut	fly
kite	throw

Story Elements—Section 5:
If You Give a Dog a Donut (page 58)
Students' drawings will vary but may include the kitchen, the apple tree, fountain, or the yard. Drawings should be labeled.

Story Elements—Section 5:
If You Give a Dog a Donut (page 59)

First   The dog will ask for some juice.
Next   The dog will go outside to pick apples.
Lastly   The dog will fly a kite.

Comprehension Assessment (pages 65–66)

1. D. take a nap
2. B. to get some muffin mix
3. The girl and the cat go in the water, build a sand castle, and look for seashells.
4. A. for some music
5. C. baseball